Blair Resources for Teaching Writing

Classroom Strategies

WENDY BISHOP
FLORIDA STATE UNIVERSITY

A Blair Press Book
PRENTICE HALL, ENGLEWOOD CLIFFS, NJ 07632

©1994 by PRENTICE-HALL, Inc.
A Paramount Communications Company
Englewood Cliffs, NJ 07632

10 9 8 7 6 5 4 3 2 1

ISBN 0-13-954199-3
Printed in the United States of America

Contents

Setting Up Your Courses

TEACHER 1:   I expected to change the lives of my students. I hoped to see major revisions in papers, students banging on my office door to discuss their papers, major concern over their writing skills. Instead, the students were friendly, likable, polite, but quite happy to do the least possible for a satisfactory grade. And who am I to say that students really should be any different? After all, I don't allow most of my professors to be major influences on me—though I've had some outstanding professors.

TEACHER 2:   I had all sorts of larger-than-life expectations which ranged from the very worst to the best. I expected my students to be narrow-minded, vacuous mouthpieces of their parents, and I expected them to have made it their semester's mission to pull every trick on me that they could. I began the semester with a "loaded for bear" mentality. I am ecstatic to say that my students have been sweethearts (and I told them so this past Monday, though I didn't use the word "sweethearts"). I've been surprised and very satisfied with how they've met the challenge of my syllabus. They accomplished the assignments well and with minimal fuss. I've been very pleased with them.

TEACHER 3:   I was surprised at how timidly I approached my 1101 class; having three years of experience should have brought me swaggering into the classroom with the confidence of a pedagogical Goliath. Some defeats, some triumphs. Some days when I felt I would make a better BMW mechanic than a teacher; others when I felt that something was taught and something (of value) was learned.

You may be reading this booklet and using *The Blair Handbook* as a new teacher of writing or as a teacher of many years' experience. You may be designing your own syllabus or have been asked to use the syllabus of your institution. Understanding that large institutional differences separate writing teachers, I hope to share with you a set of classroom strategies that have worked for other writing teachers. Since each and every reader of this booklet (and your students) has different, individual classroom contexts and needs, you should feel free to skim through the sections, finding the information you need and adapting it to your own classroom circumstances.

I opened these pages with the voices of three writing teachers to remind us that just as students bring expectations to their classrooms, so do their teachers. As teachers, we need to be aware of attitudes and how they shape classroom interactions. No matter how refined (or restrictive) the curriculum you teach, you'll have a curriculum that goes nowhere if you don't examine your views of students (eager, tricky, kids, adults, helping you, hindering you?) and your assumptions about writing classrooms (aimed at developing students' skills, aimed at developing students' fluency with academic discourse, aimed at developing students' writing processes and products?) and teachers (guides, senior learners, mentors, disciplinarians, conduits to a common knowledge base, orchestrators of classroom situations?).

Therefore, one of the first and most useful strategies you can adopt for each writing course you teach is to examine some of your assumptions. In discussion with fellow teachers or your teacher educator/supervisor, in a freewriting, or just in your head as you plan, you might want to consider these (or your own) questions.

- What are the goals and desired outcomes of the curriculum you are designing (or were hired to teach)?

- What theories of learning, writing, and reading do you think inform those goals?

- What degree of fit do you find between your beliefs about learning writing and the ways you will be teaching?

Members of some college writing programs have worked to negotiate beliefs and develop a set of (general) common principles, usually based on the research and theory of composition scholars like those listed in the bibliography at the end of this booklet. Teaching principles such as these may be developed by the director of writing, by peers who work closely together, or by a formal committee. If your institution doesn't have a set of common principles, you might use the following list, developed by the First-Year Writing Committee at my institution. Adapt, challenge, and interact with these principles as you develop your own.

First-year writing program principles

- The aim of writing and therefore the primary focus of writing instruction is discovering, shaping, and communicating meaning/ *info.*

  info, as opposed t feelings

- Students learn to write more effectively when they write for a variety of purposes, for academic as well as nonacademic audiences.

- Invention strategies help many writers get started, develop fluency, solve rhetorical problems, and reduce writing anxiety.

- Revision is an ~~essential~~ part of the writing process; multiple drafting *can* develops revision abilities.

- Frequent written or oral comments by teachers and students on writing encourage further reflecting and drafting. Comments offer

  can

  { *peer group, tutors, conferences* }

readers' responses as well as suggestions for rethinking, redrafting, and editing. *Comments after the fact are not really helpful.*

- Abundant and varied exploratory writing—in class or out of class— enhances students' abilities to write; this writing need not be graded or critiqued. *Sometimes better if not critiqued – feel of punishment inhibits some writing.*

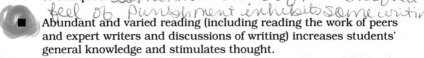

- Abundant and varied reading (including reading the work of peers and expert writers and discussions of writing) increases students' general knowledge and stimulates thought.

- Basic rhetorical and grammatical terminology provides students and teachers with a means of talking about writing strategies and about language.

■ First-year writing goals

In first- and second-term writing courses, students will work to develop their own thinking through writing; they will achieve writing fluency, clarity, and correctness through the following class activities:

- ✓ ■ learning to generate their own writing topics

- ✓ ■ writing multiple drafts of their work

- ✓ ■ writing for different audiences

- ╱ ■ contributing to the class through regular attendance and participation in peer response groups and class discussions

- ■ experiencing the research process and sharing the results of their research with the class

- ■ becoming careful readers of writing

- ■ developing an understanding of text strategies, intertextuality, and in general, a writer's knowledge of the connections between writing and reading processes

- ✓ ■ conferencing regularly with peers, teacher, and writing center tutors and developing an ability to critique their own work and the work of others

- developing an understanding of the demands of academic discourse by studying test-taking strategies and occasionally writing to set topics

- contributing a piece of writing to a class book to be produced collaboratively at the end of the semester   No.

- compiling a final class writing portfolio that showcases their class writing and class effort

- developing an ear for standard English and an improved ability to control surface correctness as demonstrated in graded papers or final portfolio drafts

If you include the most important of these program objectives and goals on your course information sheet (see page 12), your students will understand that your class consists of more than a minimum number of papers and general workshop and attendance policies.

Designing the course

Your students will generally be writing four to six papers and drafts for papers. For many teachers, the sequence of assignments is already set up. At some schools, you'll be following a modal approach, starting with narrative and descriptive essays, moving to expository drafts, and finishing with argumentative essays or research papers. More recently, composition scholars have suggested several other ways to organize a course. Briefly, I'll review a themed approach, a writing across the curriculum approach, and a writing workshop approach that allows students to develop their own drafting schedule. While I'm describing only a few courses here, you will no doubt already have designed or encountered other organizational patterns for helping students write a term's worth of essays (for instance, personal experience courses focusing on literary nonfiction essays, often autobiographical; public media courses expanding composing to considerations of news reporting, radio, and TV; reading-response courses using literary writing to prompt student writing; and so on).

Themed courses

Some courses (and many composition reading textbooks) ask students to concentrate for the entire term on a particular theme. This can be a social theme (gender issues in America, racism in America, advertising and its impact), a literary theme or genre (youth and family, the short story), or more general themes like negotiation, greed, and so on. Themed courses usually take advantage of short professional texts that address the theme. Students read and then discuss those texts and complete invention activities (freewriting, clustering, cubing, and so on), reading responses, or journal entries to discover topics of interest that they usually develop into more formal expository essays. The themed course provides the class with a common body of ideas, common readings, and related discussions but allows each writer to develop his or her own ideas in interesting ways.

Here is a shortened version of a course overview for a themed course.

COURSE OBJECTIVES AND RATIONALE:
1. To develop students' image of themselves as writers

2. To develop a better understanding of their own writing processes

3. To encourage writers to pursue a line of thinking or a particular topic over a sustained period of time

4. To use the common topic of writing about "authority"—using selected readings in a course packet and shared class writings—to help students form a community of writers who work together to create knowledge about the subject

REQUIRED MATERIALS:

Department-ordered rhetoric and handbook

"Authority" reading packet

Exploratory writing notebook

Photocopies of selected writings

ASSIGNMENT SEQUENCE:

Paper #1: Explore an experience you've had with authority as a way of identifying some of the issues you think are important to our discussion of authority.

Paper #2: Explore a time when you felt yourself developing your own sense of authority.

Paper #3: Explore an image of authority that carries some significance for you and examine the power and meaning this image holds for you.

Paper #4: Revision of papers 1, 2, and/or 3.

EXPLORATORY WRITINGS:
Rather than requiring students to keep a journal, which at times can imply that students can write privately and without restrictions, students keep an exploratory writing notebook in which they respond to issues raised by their own learning processes or by discussions of the class. These writings are rewarded for the student's thought, insight, and attempts to make meaning rather than the student's success concerning form, organization, and mechanics. Typical prompts have two main objectives. Some encourage students to explore their thinking on paper by reflecting on readings and class discussions, working to make connections between them and their personal experiences. Others give the students an opportunity to reflect on themselves as writers and their own writing processes as they become increasingly aware of those processes. Typically, writing is assigned each period, whether in class or for homework.
(Adapted from a course guide by Kim Haimes-Korn, Florida State University and Gay Lynn Crossley, Kansas State University.)

Writing across the curriculum courses

For a writing across the curriculum course, you may divide your essay topics (and accompanying readings if used) into the standard academic divisions of writing in the humanities, sciences, and social sciences. Each student may work on an essay in all areas or students may be clustered so that science majors are working on science-related essays and so on. Many teachers also include a fourth category of personal and expressive writing. Certainly both exploratory writing and research writing are important in this type of course. Class assignments that suggest ways for students to use and expand their disciplinary knowledge work well for these courses. Students may be asked to interview professionals in their field to learn writing conventions and writing practices. They may analyze journals and report on the rhetorical strategies demanded of authors who hope to submit to those journals. Often, teachers of these courses try to contact instructors in other fields, asking them to give talks to the class or perhaps even to respond to student writings from their own disciplinary perspective. (More about writing across the curriculum can be found in *Blair Resources for Teaching Writing: Writing across the Curriculum.*)

Here is a shortened version of a course overview for a writing across the curriculum course.

COURSE PURPOSES AND GOALS:
1. To introduce student writers to the importance of role playing, authority, convention, and voice in academic discourse

2. To explore the spectrum of expressive to transactional writing

3. To emphasize both reading and writing skills

The course is divided into three main units: humanities, social sciences, and natural sciences. During each unit, writers explore the characteristics of the style of writing done in that particular discipline.

REQUIRED MATERIALS:

Reader designed for writing across the curriculum

Department-ordered handbook

Photocopies of students' drafts

ASSIGNMENTS:
The course writings consist of three medium-length essays and a fourth, longer essay. Each of the first three essays deals with one of the academic areas, and the final essay takes up an area that the writer wants to explore further. One approach to this set of assignments asks students to select topics from their current course work in other departments. In another approach, the class decides on a general subject for each unit (for instance, the environment, the Vietnam War), and each student does his or her own research to narrow the topic. The final essay may ask students to choose a topic from the disciplinary area they enjoyed most or to analyze the writing in the discipline they are considering for a major.

JOURNALS:
Journals are especially important in exploring academic discourse because they can be a valuable link between private thought and public thought, course notes and expository writing. A reading-response journal based on research, lectures, and class preparation serves three functions—a chance to test dialogic inquiry, a learning log, a source of personal inquiry and self-evaluation.
(Adapted from a course overview by Cindy Wheatley-Lovoy, Florida State University.)

Writing workshop courses

I begin my own courses with a common essay assignment: to discuss one's own writing history, development of voice in writing, or writing process(es). I use this essay to teach drafting and response to writing and to develop a workshop community. While students are drafting their first essay, I ask them to contract for the semester for their other four or five papers, being sure to undertake a variety of types of writing. I base discussions of types of writing on James Britton and his colleagues' theory of discourse, which posits that most writing grows out of exploratory work (journals, extended ungraded writing, informal personal essays, and so on) and then is shaped instrumentally (primarily) to communicate in a transactional way or is shaped artistically (primarily) to communicate in an imaginative way. I ask students to develop at least one expressive topic and as an option to develop one creative/poetic topic and finally, to develop several topics in the transactional domain. If a student chooses to write poetry or fiction, he or she must always submit it with an extended process discussion—an essay that tells the story of what the writer learned by writing in an imaginative genre. I conference with all the students, helping them balance their contracts, making sure they have a challenging set of self-assigned writing projects and some good alternative topics. Also, as a class, we practice topic-generating invention exercises (these include making authority lists, developing topics from subjects of interest in other courses, brainstorming, freewriting, clustering, and so on) so students develop a pool of topic ideas. In a sense, themed courses and writing across the curriculum courses are also workshop courses, but the theme or disciplinary focus often seems to encourage the teacher to develop and assign topics. In the writing workshop course, in which students generate their own topics, I try to use writing contracts to offer guided freedom to writers.

Here is an example of a course overview of a second-semester writing workshop course that uses literary readings to prompt student responses on a variety of topics and issues.

COURSE OBJECTIVES:
To achieve writing fluency, clarity, and correctness through learning to generate writing topics, writing multiple drafts, contributing to the class through regular attendance and participation in peer response groups and class discussions, developing knowledge of the connections between writing and reading, developing the skills necessary for self-criticism, and responding to and critiquing essays written by others.

REQUIRED:
Department reader and handbook

Looseleaf paper for your journal; no notebooks or binders

Copies of first public drafts (for all five essays) and copies of one essay for the entire class

JOURNAL:
The journal will be read only by me unless announced otherwise. It should contain at least four page-long (regular margin, single-spaced) entry per week: preferably observations about your writing and

the readings in [department ordered reader] but also observations about daily life, events of significance, etc. Some entries will be assigned. Don't worry about grammar/usage/form. Drawings, paste-ins, etc. are welcome. I will read the journals at least twice during the semester and I am looking forward to reading them.

ESSAYS:

- Essays 1–4 (400–750 words each)
- Essay 5 (research paper—12,000 words)

Essays 1–4 will be reflective essays. You'll use your reading in the class reader to discover your essay topics. Reflective essays are interesting because they deal with personal observations and ideas. A reflective essay is one in which you make connections. You'll read and then reflect (think/ponder). You'll write your essay about something your pondering/reflecting led you to. The possibilities are unlimited. The important thing is how deeply you reflect/ponder. You'll be making connections between reading and life, between reading and issues/topics of interest. The more we practice making connections between things/issues/experiences, the more we exercise our reflective minds, the deeper are our mental explorations, the more we learn about ourselves and our worlds. Work hard to uncover interesting topics. Your readers will appreciate your effort. Essay 5 will be a research paper based on a topic sparked by your readings. You might want to explore, in a formal, more in-depth way, a topic or issue raised in one of your reflective essays. A separate explanation as to why you chose your topic and how it was sparked by the readings will be required. (Adapted from a course overview by William Snyder, Florida State University.)

In all these writing courses, students also are encouraged to develop and improve a paper through revision. When possible, you'll want to allow several opportunities for exploratory, in-class writing and also chances for students to individualize any assigned topic. There is a benefit for you in this; student-defined topics allow for greater writer engagement and keep a teacher from having to read twenty-five to fifty themes on the same subject.

If you grade papers individually rather than use a modified portfolio method (a discussion of portfolio grading appears in *Blair Resources for Teaching Writing: Portfolios*), consider weighting grades according to the following percentage scale:

Paper 1   10% of the final course grade
Papers 2–5   60% of the final course grade
Paper 6   10% of the final course grade

The last paper may be an in-class essay, a response to the course, etc.

Participation*   20% of the final course grade
*Participation includes invention work, drafts, participation in workshops, critiquing, etc.

This system allows you to grade on improvement and to have flexibility in assigning percentages to any one paper. For example, Bill Snyder, whose course overview I just shared for the writing workshop course, used the following proportions: Essay 1, 10% of final grade; Essays 2 and 3, each 15% of final grade; Essay 4 and Essay 5 (research paper), each 20% of final grade; Participation (discussions, critiques, etc.), 20% of final grade.

■ Journals

In many curriculums, your students will be asked to engage in exploratory writing, often in class journals. Class journals do not have to be directly linked to class assignments (although they may be linked to writing projects in progress). In journals students may explore the general strategies used to develop essays, practicing invention and topic development and writing on personally relevant issues through informal ungraded writing. Because correctness is an unimportant consideration in exploratory writing—that is, writing intended to engage ideas—teachers should not correct usage or grammar in students' journals.

Teachers should collect journals periodically, check them for completeness, and write positive comments wherever appropriate in the margins. In some classes, journals will be shared only between student and teacher. In other classes, students will share journals with peers on a regular basis. Always let your students know who their readers will be. When you read journals, it can be helpful to use a highlighter to single out vivid images, effective specifics, or interesting ideas and to add a marginal word or two to indicate exactly what is praiseworthy. Or you might set up journal reading groups of three or four class members who read and comment on each other's journals, reducing your responding load. Since journals often provide teachers with excellent formative response to classwork (students often spontaneously discuss how they feel about class activities and assignments and their own writing growth), it's wise to respond to journals *during* the semester, not just at the end of the semester. I often take home a few journals each week, respond to them, learn from them, and then collect another set; through this rotation, I can respond to each student at least twice during the term. (More about journals can be found in "*Blair Resources for Teaching Writing: Journals*".)

■ Writing conventions, writing classes, and writing centers

In many college writing programs that take a holistic approach to writing instruction, students learn to develop ideas and to communicate them by writing complete texts, developing sentence-level expertise via discussion, conferences, redrafting and revising, and careful editing of work using peer advice and handbooks as important reference tools before final class presentation of their texts. Certainly some students arrive in writing classes with underdeveloped abilities; some are unable to use the conventions of standard written English. Students who are not grammatically fluent may be seriously disadvantaged as editors of their own work or of others', and their grades will suffer if their papers are ungrammatical or incorrectly punctuated when presented for final course evaluations. These students will need individualized assignments connected to their developing text and to *The Blair Handbook* as well as additional teacher-student conferencing. In addition, if you are lucky enough to have a campus writing center, refer students there for productive, one-on-one work on individual problems in their essays. Most writing centers help students on their developing work in general, encouraging students to invent, draft, revise, and edit course assignments or personal writing with the support of a tutor.

■ First-day writing samples *(letter to instructor)*

On the first day of class, many programs require all students to complete a short piece of writing on a set or exploratory topic. Use this writing to help you decide if some students seem to be misplaced in your class or need to begin work in the writing center almost immediately. Your attitude toward and familiarity with the campus writing center makes an important difference in how willing your students may be to seek help. It's always better to walk your whole class to the facility (if your writing center is agreeable). This encourages your students to get to know the tutors and to respect the work tutors do to support them. Let students know about the center's services several times during the semester and also list the center hours in your course information sheet.

■ Course information sheets

You need not provide your students with a day-by-day syllabus specifying assignments and class activities, although you may do so. One advantage of such a syllabus is that it keeps both class and teacher on track, so the semester doesn't run out before the assignments do. One disadvantage is that it reduces the teacher's flexibility, making it harder to slow down or try a new approach when the class needs to follow a different direction than you had envisioned during week one; it also makes it harder to speed up when work goes very smoothly and a project is completed quickly. You may decide on a mixture of term-long overview and week-by-week detail. However, if you decide to do without a syllabus, you'll still want to let your students know your plans a week or two at a time, perhaps putting a new three-day plan on the board every week.

On the first or second day of the term, then, you'll need to provide students with a course information sheet specifying in unambiguous terms your policies on attendance, plagiarism, conferences, papers, basic grading procedures, and possibly manuscript form. Your information sheet should list *all* the course requirements. It should indicate the location and phone number of your office and specify your office hours. It should identify the textbooks you are using. Last, it should discuss positive aspects of the class—your goals, beliefs, and general expectations. Remember, this is the first piece of *your* writing that students read and it can sometimes set the tone for the course. I present an example of a course information sheet that can help you generate your own sheet after I review the major components of the sheet and illustrate them with samples from actual sheets.

Attendance

Regular (and prompt) attendance is usually a writing course requirement—as it must be in a course so heavily weighted toward in-class writing and peer responding. Most teachers permit students to miss two to three *hours* of class over the course of the term without penalty and begin with the fourth or fifth absence to lower the student's grade. Some teachers impose no penalty until the student's absences total a number set by a particular program as failing level. It is probably better to warn students after several absences that they are approaching grounds for failure in your course. In any event, your course information sheet should indicate precisely how many hours of absence are tolerable and what penalties will accrue for absences. Some teachers have strong feelings about tardiness. Any tardy policy you devise should be fair and be included in your policies.

During the years I've taught and advised teachers, I've found that attendance (along with grading) causes teachers the most grief. No attendance policy can make up for a curriculum that fails to engage and challenge student writers. In fact, I've sometimes found that the more detailed the attendance policy is, the more it can constrain the teacher.

You should work to be clear, to apply your policy evenly to all students, and then to get on with the more important matter of teaching writing. Here are four sample attendance policies; you'll notice that they each strike a different tone and cover department policy but also areas of particular interest to the teacher.

TEACHER A: You need to know—Class attendance and participation will count for 20 percent of your class grade. Participation includes participation in peer response groups, class discussions and other class activities, class preparation, conferences, and timely arrival to class. Department policy states that six absences is grounds for failure. You are responsible for any assignments due despite an absence. Missing a mandatory conference will be counted as an absence. Because this is a fifty-minute class, any tardiness past fifteen minutes (one-third of the class time) will be counted as an absence.

TEACHER B: Because we're a community of writers responding to and depending on one another, regular attendance, preparation, and participation are necessary. Two or more absences will affect your grade. Six hours of absences, by department policy, constitutes grounds for failure. In case of illness or emergency, call my office or home, or leave a note in my mailbox just so I know you're not taking a day off. The excused absence is a rare animal which 99 times out of 100 needs documentation.

TEACHER C: Because the class will be conducted as a workshop, your attendance and participation are important. You may have 4 absences and 5 tardies: NO EXCUSES ACCEPTED OR REQUIRED. No exceptions.

- 5th absence lowers participation grade two notches (ex., B+ to B-)

- 6th absence means FAILURE (department rule)

- Total of 6 tardies will equal one absence; 7–2, 8–3, 9–4, etc.

- Absences accumulated by tardiness will not count toward the departmental 6 absence failure rule, but they will lower your participation grade more notches.

- If you are absent, please ask a classmate for assignments (exchange telephone numbers).

PLEASE don't pack until we're finished for the period!

PLEASE if you are late, don't clomp in like a rogue Herrerasaurus!

PLEASE REFRAIN FROM TALKING WHILE OTHERS ARE TALKING!

type up own sheet to go with syllabus hours policy offices ect.

PLEASE, no eating, dipping, chewing in class. Soft drinks etc., okay. PLEASE throw away waste.

TEACHER D: This is not a course in which everything hangs on the final exam—a substantial amount of the work you have to do in order to pass will be done in the classroom. I will be looking to see your writing improve in and through the writing work we do in class. A total of six hours or more of missed classes or mandatory conferences is grounds for being failed. Each class counts as an hour, as does a conference. Late arrivals will be totaled to equal absences at my discretion. If you miss a class, it is your responsibility to find out from another member or, failing that, myself what preparation you need to do for the next lesson.

Conferences

In some programs students are required to sign up and show up for a certain number of individual conferences with the teacher. Because you will probably choose to cancel some class meetings to permit time for these conferences, the question of conference attendance should be addressed in your course information sheet. Even more, you should plan your conferencing weeks carefully. Don't schedule more than three fifteen-minute meetings in a one-hour period and more than two hours of conferencing without a significant break for yourself. Remember, conferences always run behind and you can reduce your lateness by making sure beforehand that your students know where your office is and what materials they should bring with them.

TEACHER E: Each of you is required to attend at least two individual teacher conferences. You will sign up prior to your conferences. In addition to these conferences I would like to see each of you sign up for an extra conference during my office hours. Of course, you are more than welcome to make as many additional conferences as you need. You are also welcome to stop by my office at any time during office hours.

TEACHER F: In addition to your workshop conferences, we will meet one-on-one for two regular conferences. Missing a conference counts as an absence. Also, you may make an appointment to see me, or stop by my office.

TEACHER G: Each of you will have two required conferences this semester. Please use my office hour as a chance to share writing before an assignment is due, to get feedback and inspiration when you are stuck in the writing anxiety doldrums. Don't let yourself get upset or frustrated with an assignment—talk to me first! A missed mandatory conference equals one absence. At midterm we will meet to discuss/exchange information about the course; you can give me feedback on what is working for you in the course and what isn't (if you haven't told me already) and discuss your writing goals for the rest of the semester.

Late papers

Your course information sheet should spell out the penalties, if any, for turning in work late. Some teachers permit students to turn in *one* paper late without explanation but impose a grade penalty for the second late submission. Some grant extensions on any paper due date provided the student asks in advance of that date for the extra time. Some simply drop every late paper one letter grade. The important thing is to make your own rules, whatever they are, perfectly clear to your students at the outset of the term. Those using portfolios, so that papers are not late, may decide to reduce the grades of drafts that are so incomplete as to make workshop time useless. (See *Blair Resources for Teaching Writing: Portfolios.*) If you don't set a late paper policy, students may swamp you with revised or late papers during the last week of the term. The only processes of writing they've explored then will be the processes of procrastination and single drafting.

TEACHER H: I expect you to meet deadlines for freewritings, early drafts, and final drafts. I allow you to turn in one project no more than a week late; however, it is to your benefit to remain in step with the rest of the class. You are required to inform me that the essay will be late; I am interested in your progress and do not want to lose touch with where you are in drafting and revising your project, especially since each project lasts several weeks.

TEACHER I: The development of our writing community depends on the sharing of freewritings and essays in class, on the day the writing is due. Therefore, it is important that you have your writings finished on time so you can be an active participant in the written and oral classroom dialogues. While I tend to be more sympathetic to late writing if you communicate with me before the day the writing is due, your portfolio grade will be affected if you are consistently unprepared for class.

Manuscript form

All final or portfolio drafts should be in ink, typed on a typewriter, or word-processed; you will find it easier to respond to papers that are double-spaced and on one side only of decent-quality paper. Beyond that, specify what you prefer. Some teachers find it easier to evaluate and annotate single-spaced papers that have a very wide right-hand margin, and still others insist that every shared draft be typed. Again, the essential thing is that your students understand your requirements and, even better, the thinking behind your requests.

> TEACHER J: Some informal writings and all portfolio drafts must be typed. When you format your papers, single-space your lines, leave two (2) spaces between paragraphs, and leave a 1.5-inch margin on each side. On all papers that you hand in, in the upper-left-hand corner of the first page write your name, the course number, and the date—in this order. Number each page at the top right and fasten the pages with a staple. Place a title on all papers and exploratory writing, without underlining it or placing quotation marks around it. All citation and documentation should comply with MLA style.

Plagiarism and authorship

You can use your course information sheet to address the issue of plagiarism by way of an understanding of authorship. In some programs, a plagiarized paper will be thrown out, and a substitute paper must be written to fulfill the course requirements. For instance, in my program, when a teacher is giving grades paper by paper, the substitute paper will not be graded: the student's grade on the paper in question will remain an F. The F grade is then averaged in with the other essay grades to determine the student's final grade for the course. At some institutions, plagiarism must be reported to the director of first-year writing; the director and the teacher then meet to decide whether the case will also be reported to the university judicial officer.

However, in workshop writing classes plagiarism becomes difficult to define. In fact, in some classes, collaborative writing projects are assigned. It seems necessary then that teachers discuss plagiarism, classroom definitions of individual and joint authorship, and the community contexts of sharing ideas, responding to drafts, and intervening in each other's texts. The best protection against willful or unintentional academic plagiarism is a well-run writing workshop class in which students are engaged in their own writing and the community knows each person's work and in which discussions of textuality and author's influences regularly take place.

> TEACHER K: I encourage you to share ideas and "borrow" thoughts from other students if another person's text acts as a good starting point for your own thinking/writing. According to university policy, plagiarism (which I define broadly as passing somebody else's work off as your own) constitutes grounds for failure in this course. Protect yourself by keeping all drafts of your essay, and be aware of your writing process. As personal experience and self-investment are the center of our course, turning in

a plagiarized essay acts as a grounds for failure in the course. At best you will be given an F for the paper and required to write it again; at worst you will be given an F in the course or in extreme cases be thrown to the university machinery, which could result in your being kicked out of school. You are not allowed to turn in an essay previously written for another course, although you are welcome to build upon/take apart earlier writings from other courses; just check with me about what texts you are working with and include the earlier writings as an initial draft for your thinking. Most ideas that are worthwhile will not sink in during a fourteen-week period. We will discuss the difference between "plagiarism" and "paraphrasing" around the (re)search paper time—but in general, be safe and always cite your sources.

TEACHER L: Few students actually consider plagiarizing. It's just not worth it: too much is at stake here (for instance, losing your financial aid, not being admitted to other universities or graduate school, the list goes on and on). Statistics show that most students who plagiarize are worried about their grades. Realize that the way to deal with anxiety about grades is to talk with me in the office—not to turn in someone else's work. I'm always willing to work with students to help them succeed. In this course it is OK—even helpful—to discuss your writing with other people, have them comment on your drafts or help you with proofreading your final copy. And it is OK to use spelling checkers if you have them on your word processor. Let this class be a practice arena for your future career. Learn to ask questions and ask for help. And do your own work. And know up front that in this class plagiarists will automatically fail the course and be reported to the director of first-year writing.

Sample course information sheet grid

Course Information
ENGLISH_____

Your name:
Your office number:
Your office telephone:
Your office hours:
Writing center location and hours:

COURSE OBJECTIVES:
REQUIRED MATERIALS:
(Examples: textbooks, journal notebook, photocopies of drafts, etc.)

ESSAY ASSIGNMENTS:

Paper	(Topic/Type)	Due Date
1		
2		
3		
4		
5		

Essays 1 and 2 count as ____% of final grade; essays 3, 4, and 5 count as ____% of final grade; [optional—drafts will count as ____% of final grade]; participation in workshops and in class discussions counts as ____% of final grade.

OR

PORTFOLIOS, PAPERS, AND CLASS EVALUATION

During the semester, you will be responsible for a large amount of writing, including a writing journal, ____ pieces of writing revised for the mid- and end-of-semester portfolios, a letter of self-evaluation for both portfolios, [optional—a contribution to the class book], and an in-class essay.

CLASS ACTIVITIES	WEIGHT
Journal	Satisfactory/Unsatisfactory
Class attendance and participation including peer response groups, timely arrival to class, preparation for class, conferences, and so on.	____% (suggested 30–20)
Writing—	
Midsemester portfolio	____% (suggested 70–80)
End-of-semester portfolio	____%

JOURNAL;

[Brief discussion of the way journals will be used in your class.]

LATE MATERIALS:

Students are expected to meet deadlines for invention work, early drafts, and final drafts. Failure to do so will result in a lower final essay or draft grade.

ATTENDANCE:

In a collaborative writing workshop like this, attendance is essential. If you are going to be absent and know ahead of time, please let me know, although only doctor-verified illness or grave family disturbances constitute an "excused" absence. However, excused absences really don't work because so much of your writing development will be dependent on our ongoing work together as a class. Random or spotty attendance or regularly arriving late or unprepared will indicate that you've enrolled in a class you're not prepared to complete successfully. In any event, missing a total of _____ classes and conferences is grounds for failure.

PLAGIARISM;

The work you do in this class needs to be your work, although you are encouraged to share ideas and to collaborate on projects with other writers. Save ALL your drafts to show your writing progress and to avoid worries about plagiarism. If you are ever concerned about what constitutes plagiarism, please consult me or a writing center tutor. Plagiarism is the unauthorized use of someone else's materials (a book, an article, another essay) without citing the source or the use of that work as one's own. Plagiarism is grounds for failure in the course.

SUPPLIES:

You will be responsible for some photocopying expense in order to share your writing with your peers. [Optional—Later, when we compile a class book, you will be responsible for providing 25 copies of your own work.] When someone is going to read your writing, try to type it; final (portfolio) drafts must be typed. A typed paper always receives a more comprehensive reading; it's to your benefit to provide this quality copy.

Two week schedule (Optional)

Teaching Strategies

TEACHER 4: My first week as a teacher of 1102 went very well, at least much better than I expected. The first day, I wasn't nearly as nervous as I was last semester, but the room was burning up and as I was talking I noticed a large drop of sweat dripping off my nose. I panicked for a moment, got my students writing, and ran out in the hall and wiped off my face. Wednesday we went over the policy sheet, talked about what was literature. I asked my students to read from their writing samples. It helped me to learn their names and got them used to speaking in class. After we came up with a class definition of "literature" we read the poem "Counting the Mad." The students responded to it, and then about eight students read their responses aloud. Friday was the time for our first discussion and almost everyone contributed. During the discussion we talked about ideas and several of the students said that the character reminded them of other people or themselves. We talked about there being no right interpretation. We talked about the writer's intention. I think that I pretty much taught last week like last semester. I want my students to know that I'm there to help them and that together we can find the answers because I certainly don't know all of them. Last semester I collected the journals weekly—this semester, I'll only collect them at the end of each unit, even though the students are responsible for every assignment every day. I want to see if I can trust them to do the work without me checking up on them all of the time. I've threatened them with pop quizzes if our discussions suffer, but so far they've been discussing great.

This teacher's observations make a fitting transition to the second part of this booklet—Teaching Strategies. Setting up your course may be a highly constrained matter of teaching to (or even handing out copies of) a common curriculum. What you do within the classroom is often a matter of pacing and invention, reflection and adjustment. The teacher just quoted collected first-day writing samples because her program required that she do so. However, she used those samples to introduce students and to start to build a writing community. The following sections are provided, once again, for you to adapt to your own classroom.

■ Starting the term

During the first week of class, you have a chance to set the tone for the entire term. For instance, you need to decide whether you'll have students call you by your first or your last name, whether to dress in a particular manner for class, whether to address students formally or informally, and even whether to be somewhat serious at first and let your sense of humor shine through later. At the beginning of the term, you can be sure, students will be "reading you" and comparing your class to those they've had in the past to decide how to situate themselves in this new community.

Teachers, like students, adopt different classroom roles and have different comfort levels in the classroom; some take to teaching with a great deal of apprehension and others find their teacher role relatively easy to assume. Some prefer a formal classroom, some an informal one. Twenty-two-year-old graduate teaching assistants may be worried that their eighteen-year-old students won't see them as teachers and may choose to be called by their last names, appreciating a formal distance that emphasizes their position and authority. Some teachers may choose to be called by a first name not because they are older or more experienced but because they seek when possible to inhabit peer roles in the classroom as they write exercises and papers with their classes and participate to a large degree as regular class members. Some teachers like to avoid student interest in the personal and choose to wear a type of "teaching uniform," clothes they might not normally wear. Other teachers have budgets that constrain them from being anything but what they are, individuals dressing neatly for a day's work and learning. Graduate teaching assistants often choose to dress differently on those days they are students and those they are teachers.

Overall, teachers need to create a classroom climate in which both they and their students feel comfortable, where classroom conventions—ground rules if you will—are understood, agreed upon, and fade into the background. I focus here on what may seem like small, unimportant matters—who calls whom what and simple issues of dress—because the best classroom designs may be undercut if teachers are not comfortable in their environments. And teachers who know the tenor they hope to achieve in their classroom more easily explain themselves to students, setting their students equally at ease. Since writing classrooms are often formed arbitrarily—that is, students are usually required to enroll in one of many sections of writing taught by STAFF—it seems even more important to take time during the first week to help members of that artificially formed community come to know each other.

First-week introductions

Experienced teachers often have their own favorite form of introduction activity. At the least, teachers share their course information sheet, collect a first writing sample, and read the roster, carefully checking each student's preferred name. Often teachers ask students to fill out note cards with information that helps them recall students' names and provides insight into students' past experiences in reading and writing.

For instance, on a note card I ask students to list their hometown, college major, and current phone number and address. I publish class members' phone numbers in a class roster so students can easily contact one another for outside group work, but I ask permission before doing so. Some students have valid reasons for keeping their phone numbers private.

Each term, depending on the class and my own research interests, I ask some of the following questions:

■ What other writing-related courses have you taken in the last two years?

■ What are your strengths as a writer?

■ What type of writing do you complete in or out of school? (Examples–journal, letters home, research reports, poems, etc.)

■ What do you read during a normal week?

■ What do you hope to learn from this course?

■ Tell a short story of the best or worst writing class experience from your past.

■ Tell me something about you that I wouldn't think to ask.

After students have filled out the front of a card, I ask them to exchange cards with a partner, interview that partner before introducing the partner to the class, and during that interview to find out three unusual things about the individual. They write the three things—facts, stories, insights—on the back of the note card for that individual. We go around the class introducing one another and sharing the unusual points rather than the responses to my questions. These introductions allow me to sit back and listen to the class, see individuals, and look for commonalities among them. Since introducers tend to model themselves on the first person who shares, sometimes I have to prompt class members to share more fully or to go more quickly.

Some teachers choose self-introductions, which can be equally effective and sometimes more efficient. For example, I can ask students to write down the story of how they were named (if they don't know, they can make up a story) and then to introduce themselves, sharing their story. Since names have a lot of power for all of us, these name introductions are usually quite memorable and fairly brief.

Finally, within the first week, when I have students working together in groups to share work in progress, I use the students' introduction note cards to help me memorize their names one group at a time. Many teachers also use these cards for taking roll and noting down special issues regarding individual students (learning needs, attendance problems, strong participation, etc.). Inevitably, teachers find that whatever the method used, time spent learning students' names and letting students get to know each other at the beginning of the term is time well spent in setting up a writing workshop learning community.

■ Record keeping and general organization

Every writing teacher needs to develop a method for keeping efficient records. Some writing programs provide teachers with roll books and expect all records to be kept there. Other teachers develop their own methods—like using introduction note cards for attendance records. In addition, you'll want to consider efficient methods for dealing with student journals. While there's a lot to be said for each student writing in the notebook he or she likes best, I find that it helps to ask everyone to write or word-process on 8½ by 11-inch, three-hole-punched sheets. When collecting journals, I ask only for unshared portions of each student's journal, which I place into my own three-ring binder. That way, I don't have to carry fifty pounds of notebooks around with me.

The following are some of the record-keeping decisions you'll need to make.

- ■ *Where to keep main class records.* In a roll book, on a computer, in several places to be compiled only at the end of the term? Some teachers create their own form of roll book—a binder with a sheet of paper for each student with space to include conferencing notes, observations about each paper, and so on. Some teachers also find that keeping their own class journal is a productive activity that helps them make long-range plans and predictions and provides a memory of class activities and events.

- ■ *How to protect class records from loss.* I've seen enough teachers lose a roll book to suggest that new teachers who are just figuring out their record-keeping system would do well to photocopy their records every few weeks. I also ask my students to be responsible for keeping all their papers and a record of their own attendance and participation.

- ■ *How to share class handouts—dittos and/or photocopies.* Some institutions provide dittoing services, but dittoing usually requires that you plan ahead and have your class handout prepared early. Teachers often want to use something today that they found in a student essay or journal just last night, so they tend to run up large bills at the photocopy center. When possible, ask students to provide copies for class (but also then keep your textbook costs low) and/or try to prepare teaching packets that students can purchase (see page 39 for a discussion about using teaching packets legally and ethically).

These are only a few of the organizational decisions teachers are constantly making and remaking to help keep classes running smoothly, freeing them for greater participation in discussions of writing and writers. Being efficient about the nuts and bolts of classroom operation does not mean that we as teachers are pedantic; on the contrary, efficiency on this level frees us from distraction, allowing us to be more present in the classroom without wondering in the back of our minds just where we put those papers and just when we'll have time to get the handouts made.

Emphasizing revision

Although many of us begin to revise before we put words to paper— for instance, as we take a walk we raise and then reject or accept various openings or developments for an upcoming project—most of us start revision work in earnest once we have a draft. I've drawn somewhat artificial distinctions between early and late revision and separate both those ways of looking at writing from editing, the process of preparing a final draft for submission to a teacher—essentially, publication. In describing just what a writer's fullest possible revision process might be, I present what looks like a sequence, but revision is always recursive; at any time, writers may stop and redraft, add, delete, rethink a piece. Revision is a way to invent, develop, and define; however, to get to the desired finished product, it is useful to focus on certain aspects of revision at particular times.

You'll want to develop your own classroom language for revision (zero draft, rough draft, first draft, portfolio-quality draft, and so on) because so much writing classroom time these days is spent in drafting and response sessions. Students often have underdeveloped definitions of revision and drafting and spending time on these concepts pays off in clear discussions as well as improved work.

Early revision

In early drafts, a writer is primarily involved with developing ideas while at the same time making initial decisions about what form might best communicate those ideas. In these early drafts, a writer tries out options—lots of them—options and ideas that are never seen by a reader. This happens because a writer at the beginning needs to look at the big picture and it takes some time to plot out that picture.

During early drafts, a writer is not very concerned with the fine details—mechanics, spelling, punctuation, and word choice—and that makes sense because many of the sentences the writer is using at this point won't even show up in the final draft. The writer pushes on to discover. The writer is not worried about perfection. To do this type of drafting, the writer must be flexible, try not to worry about the product, and learn to trust the process of setting out on a writing journey. To summarize, early revision may explore a writer's first conceptualization of his or her work and may take place across several drafts.

Late revision

Late revision is a relative concept. For some writers, late revision happens in the second draft and for others it happens during draft twenty-five. During late revision, a writer finalizes ideas, fits those ideas to the form he or she has chosen, and becomes concerned with smaller style options, particularly at the paragraph and sentence level. After the big picture is blocked out, it's time to look at the smaller picture of the piece, the nuances, the precise effects this text will have on an intended reader, asking, Will he or she understand or enjoy this?

During later revisions, the writer starts looking seriously at audience issues but does not become over concerned with the finest details of mechanics, spelling, and punctuation; there is still time to move a paragraph or a sentence, to think up a more effective phrase. The writer is not yet concerned with perfection but is getting close to that point. To summarize, late revision may finalize a writer's original conception for a piece and, depending on the circumstances of drafting, particularly on deadlines, may take place during drafts two to twenty or more.

Editing

It's most efficient—and generally most satisfying—to edit a piece of writing immediately before relinquishing it. When a writer gives a text to a teacher or publisher, that writer must be concerned with perfection. This is—at least momentarily—a writer's best opportunity to focus on surface-level clarity. Editing is the smallest picture of all; the writer is concerned with detail and mechanics—getting a dark print from the ribbon, setting standard margins, having a title, including his or her name, proofreading for spelling errors, checking for punctuation or grammar errors.

A writer edits so as not to alienate a reader by making the reader do the writer's work. During editing, we strive toward some standard of perfection. Editing is not a time to remove paragraphs four through seven or rewrite them, to dramatically change the genre or focus of a piece, or to add a new set of research issues.

Since editing must take place before writing is presented to other individuals for evaluation (from publishing a family Christmas card that includes a writer's poem to sharing a "public" draft in a full-class workshop to submitting final classwork to the teacher), editing is part of a writer's normal writing cycle. If a writer decides to draft an already edited piece after a period of time, he or she will expect to edit the *new version* before presenting it publicly once more.

Some writers collapse or combine parts of this sequence, depending on their writing processes, writing products, and audiences. However, it is useful to go through a full sequence several times on several pieces of writing in order to understand the value of each way of looking and looking again at a piece of written work.

Making assignments

Although many teachers are moving toward writing workshops designed to give students the greatest topic choice, many of us still ask students to write to one or more set topics or within sequenced assignments. For instance, I set the topic of the first class assignment while students are developing term contracts for papers they write during the rest of the course. Teachers often find that what seems like a clear assignment to the teacher turns out to be a baffling interpretive test to the student. Teachers often want to offer broad assignment options and students push to have the teacher say more succinctly what it is he or she "wants." Some teachers like to discuss an assignment or take students through a set of activities to prepare for an assignment, while others tend to place a task on the board and expect students to interpret the task.

Like many other teacher educators, I ask new instructors to undertake the assignments they set for their students. It can be illuminating for teachers to see how difficult a seemingly straightforward task can be; think about how you would approach the assignment "Write about the development of your own voice in writing" or "Decide what university or city issue currently affects your life the most and take a position on this issue." Every time an assignment is made, it includes a set of tacit and explicit expectations about how that assignment can best be approached, produced, and evaluated. At the least, a teacher should know how the assignment furthers his or her class goals, what a successful example of that assignment might look like (even if the teacher has never before assigned the task), what prewriting activities might help students generate a text, how much time it will take an average student to produce a successful text, and so on.

may try + write the assignment myself –

To develop effective assignments, then, you'll need to decide what the purpose of the assignment is within your own curriculum and in relation to the goals you have for that day, week, or term. Since most of us design assignments before the term, as we're planning out a term's worth of work, you should check those purposes once again when you get ready to make each assignment: Are you and your students prepared to successfully complete the assignment together? If you have never tried the assignment yourself, be particularly careful to make sure that you allow enough time for students to complete the planned work; obviously, undertaking the assignment with your students will provide you with more insight into this issue so you can better tailor the assignment for another term.

Deciding if students have enough time includes considering when and where they might best complete the assignment and what a completed product will look like. Will they share one or several drafts? Do the work inside or outside of class? Do the work by themselves or in groups with other students? Will they need to research for the project? Do they have to attend a film or campus event, view a work of art, interview an expert on their topic, and so on?

As you start to consider finished products, you'll need to decide how your students will present the work and for what audience. Certainly you can freely and specifically share your ideas on what format students will use and what conventions they must observe. Thinking about their finished products will lead you to consider how you'll evaluate those products. If you don't know your criteria because the assignment is new, be sure to brainstorm about this issue with your class, making some predictions about what products—with what qualities—the assignment might lead to. If you've made this assignment before, decide whether you want to share exemplary models of successful work or simply abstract and share the qualities of those works with your students.

There is a difference between the type of overview a teacher will write to visualize a term's writing sequence or to overview it on the course information sheet and the level of detail a teacher will want to provide when the writing assignment is made. Here are three overviews.

TEACHER M: Project 2 will focus primarily on the role relationships play in constructing our images of ourself; the essay can focus primarily on relationships and expectations in relation to body image and eating or can explore another aspect of relationships. Freewritings will take place in response to slightly longer reading assignments focusing primarily on relationships among family, friends, and boyfriends/girlfriends.

TEACHER N: In paper 1, examine why you chose your major field of study and explore the kinds of roles you picture yourself playing in that field.

TEACHER O: In essay 3, explore your social contexts, including influences of gender, race, culture, class, or geographical region. First, complete the class freewriting on the prompt "As a man/woman, I am confused about [a subject that identifies you as an individual member of a particular social group—American, teenager, native Floridian, etc.]. Then make a list of at least ten different things that confuse you about the selected topic. You'll explore this topic in further freewriting, eventually arriving at a position on one of these important issues that you can develop into an essay.

These assignment overviews lack the rich detail of a class assignment sheet, which provides the details students need if the teacher is asking them *to work toward a particular end product or to follow certain steps in their writing process.* The following assignment treats a traditional class writing topic, telling about a significant moment in a writer's life. Since the teacher has clear goals for the paper, she is right to specify them. Other teachers may prefer a less structured assignment but they should always clarify their tacit expectations about what a successful student product might look like, as this teacher does. It is easy to feel we're supportive of any direction a writer wants to take on a project; more often than not, though, we have surprisingly strong expectations for and responses to finished texts—finding them more or less acceptable according to criteria we might have made available to students.

TEACHER P: This essay will focus on one event or a series of events that tell me about you, perhaps a turning point, a moment in your life that has significance to you. Your paper will be written in first-person point of view. This unit is also part of a family unit, so I am looking for papers that deal with a family situation, one that includes at least one family member. Through the use of vivid details, narration, and/or dialogue, you will convince the reader of the event's significance.

Assignment:
Make a list of potential topics. Follow these guidelines and choose
   a) any event that involved great difficulty;
   b) any event that helped greatly to shape your personality;
   c) some "first" that gave you a new understanding of yourself or another family member;
   d) any situation in which the outcome was completely unexpected
   e) an event that you view as a turning point in your life.

include some of these ideas in essay / lecture.

Do not choose
  a) any topic from which you do not have a sufficient amount of distance—for example, do not write about the death of a parent or the abuse of a sibling if you are not comfortable doing so;
  b) any issue on which you have too great an emotional stake to make sound judgments.

And finally, ask yourself these questions:
  1. Does the event say something important about your life?
  2. Will you be able to retell the event and describe it in such a way that your readers will easily see its significance?
  3. Will the event make for an exciting or memorable story?

Part 1 of this assignment: Due January 29
This will be the first installment, in which you describe the incident or tell your memoir from your first-person point of view.

Part 2 of this assignment: Due February 5
This will also be in first-person point of view; however, this time you will be taking on the identity of someone else—another family member in the incident. This way, you may truly write a revision—you will actually be seeing the paper again through someone else's eyes, and I think it will enhance your evaluation of the event(s) and give you a new understanding of its significance. Likewise, readers will be able to see the event more completely.

Good luck, and I hope you enjoy writing your papers! Be as creative as you like—describe everything in detail. I look forward to reading all of them.

In her discussion of this assignment, the teacher offers choices, dos and don'ts, prompts for evaluating a topic choice, deadlines, an overview of interconnected parts of the assignment, an indication of how it fits into the term's work, a potential audience, and encouragement.

■ Preparing for a conference

Student-teacher writing conferences can take place informally, before, right after, or even during a class, and they can also take place by appointment in your office. The least effective conferences are those in which one or both of the confreres are poorly prepared and texts either haven't been completed, read ahead of time, or been brought along for discussion. Clearly, a little preparation can make conferences more comfortable and productive.

- When you arrange a conference, be sure your students know the time and place for the conference and if there are any special materials they should bring (portfolios, drafts, peer response sheets, etc.).

- Try to let the student know the general purpose of the conference and how long it will last. Ask them to let you know when they arrive and let them know they can expect to wait a few moments if you're busy with the preceding student.

- Ask students to formulate some questions that they have about class progress or participation and make time for them to pose those questions. *come with ideas*

Here is some advice you might offer to your students for setting up conferences with you.

- Students should remind you the day before about a conference they set up some time earlier. They should try to be clear about why they set up the conference—from discussing class progress to reviewing a recent essay—and as far ahead of the conference time as possible should provide you with a copy of a work they would like to discuss. Even if you have seen a draft earlier in the term, the writer should not expect you to remember the draft in great detail but should, instead, provide copies of early and current drafts to aid discussion.

- Writers should try to have several questions in mind and work to make the most of the conference time by being focused and prepared; writers, of course, also should be on time and call ahead if they have to change times or the conference focus.

Formats for sharing responses to writing

There is no "best" workshop method. However, there are things students and teachers can do to make sharing and responding to writing in the public forum of the classroom more productive. The following discussion can help you and your class develop its own best format. I know one teacher who sequenced his term by moving from individual work to partner work to small-group work and then to full classwork, arguing that writers are used to working alone but benefit by composing with and for larger and larger communities. I know one teacher who reversed the sequence, arguing that writers feel more comfortable sharing their work with a large group as they learn about other writers, becoming more able during that time to pick group members or partners with whom they could work. You may choose to organize your class not according to either of these broad movements, but you can see that working in different size groups will surely affect students' learning. (More about writing groups can be found in the *Blair Resources for Teaching Writing: Writing Groups*.)

Responding to a partner

Often, especially at the beginning of a writing course, you may ask students to work with one other writer. Together they can prepare class introductions, share early drafts, explore an issue and report to the class, perhaps even compose or revise a piece of writing.

Strengths: One-to-one sharing is often less intimidating than group sharing: only two people have to agree and can accomplish more. In one-to-one sharing quiet individuals gain voice, and one-to-one sharing lets individuals get to know each other quickly and fairly thoroughly.

Weaknesses: A student may get paired with someone who is difficult to work with because he or she has a different learning style, different values, or different work habits. When this happens, everyone else seems to have a better partner and the writer feels stuck in a bad learning situation.

Suggestions: Students need time to meet each other and to choose partners who share some interests. The teacher can help by mentioning learning styles and work habits and how they affect one-to-one learning; for instance, procrastinators yoked to organized performers will inevitably experience stress. Teachers can move from pair to pair trying to mediate the interactions as needed.

Responding in small groups

Small-group sharing between three to six members is common in the writing workshop. Groups may work together for an extended period of time like a unit or a full term or change membership each time the class convenes. There are benefits to both practices. When students work with the same individuals for a long period of time, they come to know each other's strengths and weaknesses and become more comfortable. At the same time, group members sometimes become too comfortable and forget to challenge each other to work to produce the best work possible. When this happens, or when one member gets restive, it is useful to have one member from each of the four or five class groups "travel" to another group. He or she will be glad for the opportunity to move on, and the group will welcome a new member and that new member's new perspective.

Strengths: Small groups can spend more time on each writer's text, allow quieter class members time to talk comfortably, get to know one another and one another's work, and build continuity from work session to work session. Small-group talk may be more supportive and less critical than large-group talk where students are trying to display their knowledge for the teacher. The teacher can only "visit" groups, so the teacher is not as likely to impose his or her taste and ideas on class members. Groups can take control of their learning and at least partially set the work pace.

Weaknesses: If group members aren't prepared, nothing gets accomplished. If some group members are too competitive, other members start to withdraw from projects and nurse grudges. If group members don't remember to invite the teacher into some of their conversations, they may lose the teacher's expertise. If groups allow one member to dominate by talking too much, imposing ideas, or slowing down the work by going off on tangents, little will be accomplished. Group work can seem to take more time to accomplish less work since each member has a voice, and understandings and agreements must be negotiated.

Suggestions: Students may be more successful if they work with people they don't know; try to avoid groupings that include best friends, romantic partners, people of the same gender, and so on. Emphasize preparation and timeliness so group time is really work time. Ask members to evaluate their own participation during a freewriting session: who is talking enough and who is talking too much, and so on? Help groups set up necessary member duties: at a minimum, groups need a *timekeeper* who helps ensure that each member's work is discussed. Groups may need a group *historian* who takes notes on a discussion and shares them later with the full class. Last but not least, a *general group member* helps facilitate all these activities. And no one should always take the same role; encourage your students to exchange roles and expand their capabilities.

Responding as a class

In any writing workshop, some time will be devoted to full-class sharing. Although some students seem to prefer small-group sharing and others full-class sharing, there are beneficial aspects to both and most teachers develop their own best balance. Without exception, class writers seem to feel that critiquing the work of peers is difficult but, ultimately, rewarding, and the full-group sessions usually run more smoothly if the teacher trains students in preferred models of response.

Strengths: Full-group response sessions provide writers with the largest possible number of responses, increasing their ability to understand audience(s) and discover revision directions. Usually a full-class response session raises conflicting views, encouraging writers to think more deeply about their writing goals. When directing a full-class session, the teacher can be sure that important points are covered, that each writer receives attention, that no writer dominates the discussion, and that the teacher's expertise is shared. Full-class sharing makes efficient use of limited class time.

Weaknesses: Full-group sharing means that fewer pieces of writing are covered and often those that are covered are discussed only briefly. For some writers, the contradictory responses they receive in a full-class response session may seem unsupported, making it difficult to respond to any of them. Teachers have to be careful not to let certain vocal students dominate the discussion and to avoid dominating the discussion themselves. Shy students may feel they don't dare speak. It may be complicated to copy and circulate the required samples of work for each workshop. The teacher may be too controlling about the direction discussions take.

Suggestions: Students need to be encouraged to read the workshop manuscripts ahead of time and write notes for the writers, to volunteer responses quickly, and to share ideas in detail and then allow others to share ideas. Writers need to be encouraged to treat other writers the way they hope to be treated themselves, to share feelings about the directions the workshops take, and to be active members.

also good for peer evaluation

Guiding peer response to class writing   *guidelines*

The following questions were designed for guiding peer response to a writer's original work. In any writing class you teach, you'll find it helpful to train students in ways of responding, whether that response takes place between partners, among small-group members, or within a full-class workshop. You can have the class help you set up response guidelines or rules or simply share the guidelines you choose to follow and even model those guidelines by conducting a practice response session using student papers from a previous term. If you're teaching for the first time, you should be able to find colleagues at your institution who would be willing to share a set of papers for this purpose.

My own response guidelines change each year. These are a recent variation. For these workshops, essays were available ahead of discussion periods.

1. Each writer will read a paragraph aloud.

2. All class members will share in the discussion.

3. Try to offer the writer a sense of how you read the piece. Among many other things, you might tell him or her how you understood or enjoyed the text; what sentence or image seemed crucial to the text and your understanding of it (essentially, identify the center of gravity); where your attention lagged (and perhaps picked up again); how you felt as the audience for this piece (were you the right audience? do you need to know more about the writer's intended audience? and so on), where you felt gaps, wished for more, felt something was being held back, and so on.

4. Try to offer the writer a sense of possible revision directions. Among other things, you might tell him or her how to lengthen or shorten the piece, if the beginning and ending are effective, and so on; how he or she could experiment in a way you'd find interesting; if you sense any risk taking going on and how to keep capturing that sense of working dangerously (but also productively); where breaking the conventions does work (usage, sentence structure, invented words, punctuation, etc.) and/or where you're worried by broken conventions (are they intentional? ineffective?).

5. Try to offer the writer insight into his or her prose style. Among other things, you might tell him or her what you notice about word choice; which sentences are effective (and why) and which ones are choppy, tangled, confusing, or so on; about the strategies you notice (metaphorical language, repetition, balance, circular movement, self-consciousness, etc.); suggest whether these strategies should be used more or less often; about style or technique by saying how the writer's prose differs or seems similar to your own.

6. You cannot say there is nothing to say. All writings in this class can be studied and should, through our suggestions, be strengthened. Your comments will help other class writers challenge themselves.

Responding to student writing

A great deal of research has been conducted in the last few years to help teachers learn how best to respond to student writing. The subject is so large that I can only sketch out issues that might arise for teachers who hope to improve their response styles; there are useful related works in this area in the bibliography.

At the least, you'll want to consider the following.

1. Your overall method of responding and grading student writing. Will you grade papers as they are submitted or develop a portfolio evaluation system (discussed in *Blair Resources for Teaching Writing: Portfolios*).

2. How will you explore and deal with the inevitable subjectivity that accompanies the act of responding to or grading writing? When you assign work, do you have an idea of what a successful piece of writing looks like?

3. How will you respond to student writers most effectively? Will you respond to early, late, or final drafts? How often and in what degree of detail? *conference + final draft*

4. How will you respond to writing most efficiently? Will you write on the text or off the text, respond with corrections or summative end-notes or both? Will you vary your responding style by assignment or work to develop a single style?

5. How do you come across in your responses to students? Are you supportive, directive, reflective, and so on? Do students understand your responses and benefit from them?

These are only a few of the questions teachers (and students) ask about responding, and you'll benefit from sharing sample papers with a teaching supervisor or office colleagues to discuss response and grading issues. Although most programs train teachers in a preferred way of responding and grading, you will find that grading occupies much of your teaching time and that, inevitably, you'll need to consider grading and response often and will benefit from exploring grading issues on your own.

■ Encouraging student responses to your course

It's very easy to assume the worst about your writing classes. At 8:00 A.M., a class can fail to respond to an activity that you stayed up late preparing. Or, after you return evaluated papers, the swift movement of students to the last page of their papers to examine the grade (or the even more disconcerting tossing of papers into book bags) can make you worry about students' investment in the class and your effectiveness as a teacher. Many times you can't quite figure out if the day's work was a success or a failure. The best way to obtain a better picture of your class is to ask students to respond throughout the semester—providing you with formative evaluations of the class and their participation in the class. You can also learn a lot about students' developing understanding of writing processes—traces of which aren't always discernible in final drafts—by asking a series of questions about their composing habits early and late in the term and by asking for a process cover sheet that tells the story of composing each finished product.

The following are some suggestions for eliciting and encouraging student response.

1. Early in the course ask students to respond to questions related to your teaching goals and then have them complete the same activity at the end of the term. Compare their early and late writings. Questions might include. What is your writing process? What is good writing? What is the connection between reading and writing? And so on.

2. When you return a set of papers with a response or a grade, ask students to freewrite for a few moments in response to your response. Where were you clear or unclear? How do they feel about their class progress to date? What could they apply from this draft to their next draft? And so on.

3. After you've given an assignment, ask students to write for a few minutes about confusions they may feel or questions they have. Take these anonymous responses and read them to the class, asking class members to answer the questions when possible.

4. After students have worked in small response groups (or shared workshop responses as a full class) ask them to analyze the dynamics of their group or of the class. What worked, what didn't? What could you do next time to improve their learning?

5. As students draft a text, ask them to keep journal notes recording their exact activities; when they submit a final copy of the paper, ask them to submit a process cover sheet that tells the story of what happened and what they feel they learned during the course of writing the text.

6. Before students move from one draft to another, ask them to write about what is involved in their successful completion of the text. Are they facing a big test or visit from a relative that interferes with quiet writing time? Are they unsure about the next thing they should do in their draft? And so on. You might also ask them to sketch out a time line that shows how they could complete their work successfully and ask them to try to stick to that time line.

You can see that there are many ways to use writing to help you better gauge the progress of your class. Don't imagine the worst; ask those who know best—the students in your class (and try writing with them to explore your own feelings). Through their written responses, you'll have a better measure than tired faces for deciding how to structure your next class period, drafting sequence, or term.

■ Using teaching packets

At many institutions, teachers need or want to augment a required textbook with a teaching packet. Making a packet can embroil you in certain problems, however, so you need to explore the ethical and legal issues. When compiling teaching packets, writing teachers are able to use materials they have designed. When a single class text is used, students also can be expected to purchase a small teaching packet *and* to undertake the expense of copying their own writing for class workshops. Teachers should warn students of the approximate costs of teaching packets and photocopying in their course information sheet and should try to keep these costs as low as possible.

The following are some suggestions for putting together a teaching packet.

1. Respect copyright laws; reproduce only limited materials from other sources. Find out how to request permission to reprint (the copy shop may be able to help) and start the request process early. Avoid reproducing materials that already exist in *adequate* versions in your required textbooks.

2. Materials gathered from various sources can be paraphrased— *observing appropriate documentation*—to ensure coherence and to provide discussions students can understand, keep, and reuse. For most teachers, the formal presentations in *The Blair Handbook* should suffice.

3. Selecting professional essays as models to encourage writing in modes or forms often proves restrictive to student writers. Students need, when possible, to discover the requirements of writing through writing. When using sample essays, include student writing. And although essays may serve for writing discussions, they should be connected also to written response activities—journal entries, in-class directed writings, analyses of writers' choices, and so on.

4. For activities such as grammar reviews or editing lessons, create a ditto of sample sentences derived from real problem sentences found in current class essays. Activities or exercises often lose relevance and power when they continue, canned, from semester to semester.

5. Include student work (prewriting, drafts, and revisions) that illustrates writing in progress. These samples may include flawed as well as exemplary pieces.

6. Include class policies; grading/evaluation rubrics (developed by you or by your previous classes); sample evaluated papers that illustrate your response methods or that model effective and/or destructive response styles for peer group training; and so on.

7. Include a *few* process or usage discussions *that you have written* into a format you prefer (using nonthreatening vocabulary, institution-specific references and examples, and so on).

8. As a variation, ask students to compile a class packet, each writer contributing one of his or her essays. Ask students to find, analyze, and share types of writing they value and compile a second class packet part way through the semester if you can obtain copyright permission.

Teaching packets offer you a chance to design a responsive and responsible writing course. Other teachers often have samples of successful packets that they can share with you. Before you begin making your packet, read the Education and Fair Use Federal Copyright Law and contact your local copy shop for their advice on compiling successful classroom packets. Realize that in recent years this law has been interpreted in increasingly strict ways. While copy shops will help you obtain permissions from authors, passing the costs on to your students, the costs of permission may make your packet costs prohibitively high for your students.

■ Troubleshooting, daily problems, asking for help

All teachers depend on their supervisors and community of peers to help them decide how to react to the variety of classroom problems, surprises, and issues that can develop in any writing program. We all ask questions about our teaching, all the time: What do we do when students pack their bags and walk out the door before class is over, when a student paper or journal touches on life experiences that make us worry about the student's emotional or physical well-being, when students test our stated limits by pushing a late-paper or attendance policy, when a class activity fails to work, or even a semester's work seems less effective than it should have been?

Because students are generally required to take first-year writing courses, they naturally resist the course and sometimes the teacher who is teaching it (that teacher, in turn, may feel less than fully supported by an institution that offers only part-time, GTA, or adjunct contracts). New teachers particularly are worried about presenting themselves authoritatively and maintaining students' respect. To do this, they need to do their own homework, of course, participating in all teacher education opportunities open to them. They should work to share their concerns with their supervisors and peers and they will find it useful to work through prospective areas of difficulty themselves. What will they do with a peer group that refuses to settle down to a task, with three students who sit in a corner and talk to each other during full-class discussion, with the student who never comes to class with a draft in hand, with the student who has started to miss every Friday class, with the student who bursts into tears in an office conference, and so on. Even more, how do these student behaviors play out issues of authority, autonomy, and community?

Many teachers talk about students who bring "high school" behavior to the college classroom. Some teachers choose to address a class discussion early in the term to the changes students will experience coming to college classrooms: for instance, students, not their parents, are now in charge of the alarm clock and of activities that take place the night before. Some teachers make a point of responding to disruptive behavior immediately, in front of the whole class. Others need to figure out their feelings and tell the class the next time what limits and rules need to be in effect to support the work of the community. Still others choose to let the class out a few minutes early but hold certain students behind for a discussion, asking them to refrain from the problematic behavior in the future (and why). I suggest that teachers choose the option that doesn't back them into a corner of needing to "save face," that lets them remain flexible and responsive as they investigate a student's motivations and their own strong reaction to the student's behavior. This means that teachers will want to take time to find out in conferences what students are experiencing and thinking. If a teacher publicly castigates a student for being tardy and threatens him or her with a punishment the next time it happens, and then it happens, the punishment is inevitable. But a short talk with the student can turn up reasons for the behavior (from roommate hazing to family problems) that may be addressed more effectively in private. It is important to remember that teachers are not parents and that students are maturing adults who need to take (and be given) responsibility for their own behavior. This is not to say that private discussion will solve all classroom behavior problems. In fact, every teacher, at some time in his or her teaching career, needs to call in a supervisor for advice.

Additionally, you'll often encounter students with special needs. Sometimes students will tell you about these and sometimes you'll discover them by accident. Most campuses provide support for students with physical and learning disabilities and for students undergoing emotional stress who find themselves in need of professional counseling. Also, for many of our students, English may not be a first language and both U.S. and college cultures can prove new or problematic for some of them. (More about this can be found in "*Blair Resources for Teaching Writing: English as a Second Language.*")

You'll want to develop responses to a set of stock situations: the student who "must have an A in your class," who claims he or she didn't hear the assignment, who comes by your office innumerable times to be sure he or she is "doing it right," who swears he or she slipped an overdue draft under your office door, who complains because you haven't gotten papers graded or returned yet, who has a perpetually broken alarm clock *and* your eight o'clock class, and so on. Having clearly articulated policies in a course information sheet helps clarify some of these issues. On-the-spot informal counseling (suggestions to buy a new alarm clock, assuring a student that he or she is making necessary progress) and developing new class policies (papers can be turned in only during class or to a department late-paper file, announcing your estimated schedule for returning papers and updating it each class, handing out an updated assignment schedule at the beginning of each class, and so on) can also help.

It's inevitable, though, that every time you troubleshoot one class situation, two more may spring up, but realize that these problems fall into recognizable categories (classroom behavior, student life problems, flaws in a curriculum that can be remedied during the next term) and that paying attention to the ones you experience will improve your next class. If your teaching apprehensions center in this area, you might find it useful to purchase a copy of *Scenarios for Teaching Writing: Contexts for Discussion and Reflective Practice* by Chris Anson and his colleagues (Urbana: NCTE, 1993); these authors don't provide pat answers but they do provide you with a variety of useful, actual classroom cases that you can reflect on before they occur—or to keep them from occurring—in your own classroom.

■ Joining the professional community

This booklet only begins to share samples of the wealth of information about classroom teaching strategies that you can obtain from your own teaching colleagues. Every teacher can recall curricular and personal events that played out well or ill, that the teacher has contemplated over the years, working to improve an aspect of his or her classroom the next time a similar issue arises. In a way, these moments are all part of an important body of teacherlore—those stories teachers share to help one another improve instruction and to endure sometimes problematic teaching conditions. I'm certain that in a very short while, you could compile a list of your own strategies like the ones I've presented here simply by interviewing colleagues at your institution.

Equally, teachers look to their program administrator for advice and to professional organizations like the Conference on College Composition and Communication and the National Council of Teachers of English. Through membership dues, these organizations finance journals (*College English, Research in the Teaching of English, College Composition and Communication, Teaching English in the Two-Year College*) and host annual conventions where you can meet with other teachers to share advice, augment your teaching, and work to improve your institutional conditions. You can obtain information on membership, journal subscriptions, and conferences by writing to National Council of Teachers of English, 1111 Kenyan Road, Urbana, IL 61801; phone: (800) 369-6283.

In a similar way, many of the works listed on the Bibliography will support your teaching and offer an entry into the professional community of composition and rhetoric.

Bibliography: For Further Reading

These readings *do not* represent a comprehensive introduction to composition and rhetoric. But they are representative of readings that have guided my own teaching as well as the composition of this booklet. If you are a new teacher with limited funds but are interested in compiling your own teaching library, I'd suggest you begin with those entries that I have starred (*).

CCC = *College Composition and Communication*
CE = *College English*
JAC = *Journal of Advanced Composition*
MLA = *Modern Language Association*
RTE = *Research in the Teaching of English*
ERIC = *ERIC Document Reproduction Service*
NCTE = *National Council of Teachers of English*
SIUP = *Southern Illinois University Press*
B/C-H = *BOYNTON/COOK-HEINEMANN*

Computer-assisted composition

Duin, Ann Hill, and Kathleen S. Gorak, eds. *Writing with the Macintosh Using Microsoft Word.* Cambridge, MA: Course Technology, 1991.

*Hawisher, Gail, and Cynthia Selfe, eds. *Evolving Perspectives on Computers and Composition Studies: Questions for the 1990s.* Urbana: NCTE, 1991.

*Holdstein, Deborah, and Cynthia L. Selfe. *Computers and Writing: Theory, Research, Practice.* New York: MLA, 1990.

Mitchell, Joan P. *Writing with a Computer.* Boston: Houghton, 1989.

Selfe, Cynthia L., Dawn Rodriques, and William R. Oates, eds. *Computers in English and the Language Arts.* Urbana: NCTE, 1989.

Tuman, Myron C. *Writing with Norton Textra: A Guide for Composing On-Line.* New York: Norton, 1991.

Institutional and rhetorical history

Applebee, Arthur N. *Tradition and Reform in the Teaching of English: A History.* Urbana: NCTE, 1974.

*Berlin, James A. *Rhetoric and Reality: Writing Instruction in American Colleges, 1990—1985.* Carbondale: SIUP, 1987.

_____. *Writing Instruction in Nineteenth-Century American Colleges.* Carbondale: SIUP, 1984.

_____. "Writing Instruction in School and College English, 1890—1985." *A Short History of Writing Instruction: From Ancient Greece to Twentieth-Century America.* Ed. James J. Murphy. Davis, CA: Hermagoras, 1990. 183–220.

*Bizzell, Patricia, and Bruce Herzberg. *The Rhetorical Tradition: Readings from Classical Times to the Present.* Boston: Bedford, 1990.

*Bullock, John, and John Trimbur. *The Politics of Writing Instruction.* Vol. 2. Portsmouth, NH: B/C-H, 1990.

*Graff, Gerald. New York. *Beyond the Culture Wars: How Teaching the Conflicts Can Revitalize American Education.* Norton, 1992.

_____. *Professing Literature: An Institutional History.* Chicago: U of Chicago P, 1987.

*LeFevre, Karen Burke. *Invention as a Social Act.* Carbondale: SIUP, 1987.

*Greenblatt, Stephen, and Giles Gunn, eds. *Redrawing the Boundaries: The Transformation of English and American Literary Studies.* New York: MLA, 1992.

Knoblauch, C.H., and Lil Brannon. *Rhetorical Traditions and the Teaching of Writing.* Montclair, NJ: B/C, 1984.

Theory and pedagogy

Anderson, Chris. *Literary Nonfiction: Theory, Criticism, Pedagogy.* Carbondale: SIUP, 1989.

*Bartholomae, Davie. "Inventing the University." *When a Writer Can't Write.* Ed. Mike Rose. New York: Guilford, 1985. 134–65.

Beach, Richard. *A Teacher's Introduction to Reader-Response Theories.* Urbana: NCTE, 1993.

Belenky, Mary Field, Blyth McVicker Clinchy, Nancy Rule Goldberger, and Jill Mattuck Tarule. *Women's Ways of Knowing: The Development of Self, Voice, and Mind.* New York: Basic, 1986.

Berthoff, Anne E. *The Making of Meaning: Metaphors, Models, and Maxims for Writing Teachers.* Upper Montclair, NJ: B/C, 1981.

Bishop, Wendy, and Hans Ostrom, eds. *Colors of a Different Horse: Rethinking Creative Writing, Theory, and Pedagogy.* Urbana: NCTE, forthcoming.

Caywood, Cynthia L., and Gillian Overing, eds. *Teaching Writing: Pedagogy, Gender, and Equity.* Albany: State of New York P, 1987.

*Crowley, Sharon. *A Teacher's Introduction to Deconstruction.* Urbana: NCTE, 1989.

*Crusius, Timothy. *Discourse Theories: A Critique and Synthesis of Major Theories.* New York: MLA, 1989.

Dean, Terry. "Multicultural Classrooms, Monocultural Teachers." *CCC* 40 (1989): 23–37.

*Eagleton, Terry. *Literary Theory: An Introduction.* Minneapolis: U of Minneapolis P, 1983.

*Elbow, Peter. *Embracing Contraries: Explorations in Learning and Teaching.* New York: Oxford UP, 1986.

Flynn, Elizabeth. "Composing as a Woman." *CCC* 39 (1988): 423–35.

Gilligan, Carol. *In a Different Voice: Psychological Theory and Women's Development.* Cambridge: Harvard UP, 1982.

Harkin, Patricia, and John Schilb, eds. *Contending with Words: Composition and Rhetoric in a Postmodern Age.* New York: MLA, 1991.

*Lindemann, Erika. *A Rhetoric for Writing Teachers.* 2nd ed. New York: Oxford UP, 1987.

Moi, Toril. *Sexual/Textual Politics: Feminist Literary Theory.* London: Methuen, 1985.

Moxley, Joseph, ed. *Creative Writing in America: Theory and Pedagogy.* Urbana: NCTE, 1989.

*Murray, Donald. *Expecting the Unexpected: Teaching Myself—and Others—to Read and Write.* Portsmouth, NH: B/C, 1989.

*_____. *Learning by Teaching: Selected Articles on Writing and Teaching.* Upper Montclair, NJ: B/C, 1982.

_____. *A Writer Teaches Writing.* Boston: Houghton, 1968.

Rich, Adrienne. *On Lies, Secrets, and Silence: Selected Prose, 1966– 1978.* New York: Norton, 1979.

*Scholes, Robert. *Textual Power: Literary Theory and the Teaching of English.* New Haven: Yale UP, 1985.

Scholes, Robert, Nancy R. Comley, and Gregory L. Ulmer. *Textbook: An Introduction to Literary Language.* New York: St. Martin's, 1988.

Smith, Frank. "Myths of Writing." *Language Arts* 58 (1981): 792–98.

Winterowd, W. Ross. *The Rhetoric of the "Other" Literature*. Carbondale: SIUP, 1990.

■ Writing across the curriculum

Britton, James, T. Burgess, N. Martin, A. McLeod, and H. Rosen, *The Development of Writing Abilities, 11—18*. London: Macmillan, 1975.

Emig, Janet. "Writing as a Mode of Learning." *CCC* 28 (1979): 122–28.

Gere, Ann Ruggles, Ed. *Roots in the Sawdust: Writing to Learn across the Disciplines*. Urbana: NCTE, 1985.

Griffin, C.W. "Programs for Writing across the Curriculum: A Report." *CCC* 36 (1985) 398–403.

Herrington, Anne, and Charles Moran, eds. *Writing, Teaching, and Learning in the Disciplines*. New York: MLA, 1992.

Knoblauch, Cy, and Lil Brannon. "Writing as Learning through the Curriculum." *CE* 45 (1983): 465–74.

Tchudi, Steven. *Teaching Writing in the Content Areas*. National Educational Association, Washington, D.C., 1986.

*Young, Art, and Toby Fulwiler. *Writing across the Disciplines*. Upper Montclair, NJ: B/C, 1986.

■ Writing apprehension

*Daly, John A. "Writing Apprehension." *When a Writer Can't Write*. Ed. Mike Rose. New York: Guilford, 1985. 134–65.

Hartwell, Patrick. "Creating a Literate Environment in Freshman English: How and Why." *Rhetoric Review* 6 (1987): 4–21.

McAndrew, Donald. "Writing Apprehension: A Review of Research." *Research and Teaching in Developmental Education* 2 (1986): 43–52.

Murray, Donald M. "The Essential Delay: When Writer's Block Isn't." *When a Writer Can't Write*. Ed. Mike Rose. New York: Guilford, 1985. 219–26.

Rose, Mike. "Rigid Rules, Inflexible Plans, and the Stifling of Language: A Cognitive Analysis of Writer's Block." *CCC* 31 (1980): 389–99.

■ Writing groups and the writing workshop

Bishop, Wendy. *Released into Language: Options for Teaching Creative Writing.* Urbana: NCTE, 1990.

_____.*Peer Groups: An Annotated Bibliography.* "Research, Theory, and Pedagogy of Writing." 1987. ERIC 276 035.

*Brooke, Robert E. *Writing and Sense of Self: Identity Negotiation in Writing Workshops.* Urbana: NCTE, 1991.

Bruffee, Kenneth A. "Collaborative Learning and the Conversation of Mankind." *CE* 46 (1984): 635–52.

_____. "Writing and Reading as Collaborative or Social Acts." *The Writer's Mind: Writing as a Mode of Thinking.* Ed. Janet L. Hays et al. Urbana: NCTE, 1983.

Ede, Lisa, and Andrea Lunsford. *Singular Texts/Plural Authors: Perspectives on Collaborative Writing.* Carbondale: SIUP, 1990.

*Elbow, Peter. *Writing without Teachers.* New York: Oxford UP, 1977.

*_____. *Writing with Power.* New York: Oxford UP, 1981.

*Elbow, Peter, and Pat Belanoff. *Sharing and Responding.* New York: Random, 1989.

*Gere, Ann Ruggles. *Writing Groups: History, Theory, and Implications.* Carbondale: SIUP, 1987.

*Harris, Joseph. "The Idea of Community in the Study of Writing." *CCC* 40 (1989): 11–22. Rpt. in Richard Graves, ed. *Rhetoric and Composition.* 3rd ed. Portsmouth, NH: B/C-H, 1992. 267–78.

*Harris, Muriel. *Teaching One-to-One: The Writing Conference.* Urbana: NCTE: 1986.

Weiner, Harvey S. "Collaborative Learning in the Classroom: A Guide to Evaluation." *CE* 48 (1986): 52–61.

Wilbers, Stephen. *The Iowa Writers' Workshop: Origins, Emergence, and Growth.* Iowa City: U of Iowa, 1981.

■ Writing journals

Deckert, Andrew J. "Keeping a Teacher's Writing Journal." *English Journal* 77 (Feb. 1988): 48–50.

*Fulwiler, Toby, ed. *The Journal Book.* Upper Montclair, NJ: B/C, 1988.

Mayher, John S., Nancy Lester, and Gordon M. Pradl. *Learning to Write/Writing to Learn.* Upper Montclair, NJ: B/C, 1983.

Newman, Judith M. "Sharing Journals: Conversational Mirrors for Seeing Ourselves as Learners, Writers, and Teachers." *English Education* 20 (Oct. 1988): 134–56.

■ Writing process: theory, research, practice

Anson, Chris, Joan Graham, David A. Jolliffee, Nancy S. Shapiro, and Carolyn H. Smith, eds. *Scenarios for Teaching Writing: Contexts for Discussion and Reflective Practice.* Urbana: NCTE, 1993.

Bartholomae, David, and Anthony R. Petrosky. *Facts, Artifacts, and Counterfacts.* Upper Montclair, NJ: B/C, 1986.

Bishop, Wendy. *Something Old, Something New: College Writing Teachers and Classroom Change.* Urbana: CCCC/NCTE, 1990.

*_____. ed. *The Subject Is Writing: Essays by Teachers and Students.* Portsmouth, NH: B/C-H, 1993.

_____. "Writing Teachers and Writing Process: Combining Theory and Practice". *Arizona English Bulletin* 29.3 (1987): 34–41.

Bridwell-Bowels, Lillian S. "Revision Strategies in Twelfth Grade Students' Transactional Writing." *RTE* 14 (Oct. 1980): 197–222.

*Cooper, Marilyn. "The Ecology of Writing." *CE* 31 (1986): 134–42.

Emig, Janet. *The Composing Processes of Twelfth Graders.* Urbana: NCTE, 1971.

*Faigley, Lester. "Competing Theories of Process." *CE* 48 (1986): 527–42.

Flower, Linda. "Writer-Based Prose: A Cognitive Basis for Problems in Writing." *CE* 41 (1981): 19–37.

Flower, Linda, and John R. Hayes. "A Cognitive Process Theory of Writing. *CCC* 32 (1981): 365–87.

*Graves, Richard, ed. *Rhetoric and Composition.* 3rd ed. Porstmouth, NH: B/C-H, 1992.

Harste, V. C., V.A. Woodward, and C. L. Burke, *Language Stories and Literacy Lessons.* Portsmouth, NH: Heinemann, 1984.

Heath, S. B. *Ways with Words: Language, Life, and Work in Communities and Classrooms.* New York: Cambridge UP, 1983.

Hurlbert, Mark, and Samuel Totten, eds. *Social Issues in the English Classroom.* Urbana: NCTE, 1992.

Lindemann, Erika. *A Rhetoric for Writing Teachers*. 2nd ed. New York: Oxford UP, 1987.

Murray, Donals. "Writing as Process: How Writing Finds Its Own Meaning." *Eight Approaches to Teaching Composition*. Ed. Timothy Donovan and Ben McClelland. Urbana: NCTE, 1980 3–20.

*Newkirk, Thomas, ed. *Nuts and Bolts: A Practical Guide to Teaching College Composition*. Portsmouth, NH: B/C-H, 1993.

Ponsot, Marie, and Rosemary Deen. *Beat Not the Poor Desk*. Upper Montclair, NJ: B/C, 1982.

Perl, Sandra. "The Composing Process of Unskilled College Writers." *RTE* 13 (1979): 317–36.

Pianko, Sharon. "A Description of the Composing Processes of College Freshman Writers." *RTE* 13 (1979): 5–22.

*Ronald, Kate, and John Volkmer. "Another Competing Theory of Process: The Students'." *JAC* 9 (1989): 81–96.

*Shaughnessy, Mina P. *Errors and Expectations: A Guide for the Teacher of Basic Writing*. New York: Oxford UP, 1977.

*Smith, Frank. *Writing and the Writer*. New York: Holt, 1983.

Sommers, Nancy. "Revision Strategies of Student Writers and Experienced Adult Writers." *CCC* 31 (1980): 378–88.

*Tate, Gary, and Edward P. J. Corbet, eds. *The Writing Teacher's Sourcebook*. New York: Oxford UP, 1981.

*Tobin, Lad. *Writing Relationships*. Portsmouth, NH: B/C-H, 1993.

Writing portfolios and writing assessment

*Anson, Chris M. *Writing and Response: Theory, Practice, and Research*, Urbana: NCTE, 1989.

Bartholomae, David. "Writing Assignments: Where Writing Begins." *Fforum*. Ed. Patricia Stock. Upper Montclair, NJ: B/C, 1983. 300–12.

Beavan, Mary H. "Individualized Goal Setting, Self-Evaluation, and Peer Evaluation." *Evaluating Writing: Describing Measuring, Judging*. Ed. Charles R. Cooper and Lee Odell. Urbana: NCTE, 1977. 135–56.

*Belanoff, Pat, and Marcia Dickson, eds. *Portfolio Grading: Process and Product*. Portsmouth, NH: B/C-H, 1991.

Bishop, Wendy. "Designing a Writing Portfolio Evaluation System." *English Record* 40.2 (1990): 21–25.

Burnham, Christopher C. "Portfolio Evaluation: Room to Breathe and Grow." *Training the New Teacher of College Composition.* Ed Charles Bridges. Urbana: NCTE, 1986. 125–38.

Fuller, David. "A Curious Case of Our Responding Habits: What Do We Respond to and Why?" *JAC* 8 (1988): 88–96.

Graves, Donald. "Break the Welfare Cycle: Let Writers Choose Their Topics." *Fforum.* Ed. Patricia Stock. Upper Montclair, NJ: B/C, 1983. 98–101.

Elbow, Peter, and Pat Belanoff. "Portfolios as a Substitute for Proficiency Examinations." *CCC* 37 (1986): 336–39.

Hartwell, Patrick. "Grammar, Grammars, and the Teaching of Grammar." *CE* 47 (1985): 105–27.

Knoblauch, C. H., and Lil Brannon. "Teacher Commentary on Student Writing: The State of the Art." *Freshman English News* 10 (Fall 1981): 1–4.

Larson, Richard. "Making Assignments, Judging Writing, and Annotating Papers: Some Suggestions." *Evaluating Writing: Describing, Measuring, Judging.* Ed Charles R. Cooper and Lee Odell. Urbana: NCTE, 1977. 109–16.

Lindemann, Erika. "Making and Evaluating Writing Assignments." *A Rhetoric for Writing Teachers.* New York: Oxford UP, 1987. 191–223.

"Portfolio Assessment: An Annotated Bibliography." *Quarterly* 10 (Oct. 1988): 23–24.

*White, Edward. *Teaching and Assessing Writing.* San Francisco: Jossey-Bass, 1988.

Williams, Joseph M. "The Phenomenology of Error." *CCC* 32 (May 1981): 152–68.

◾ Writers on writing

Coltelli, Laura, ed. *Winged Words: American Indian Writers Speak.* Lincoln: U of Nebraska P, 1990.

Murray, Donald. *Shoptalk: Learning to Write with Writers.* Portsmouth, NH: B/C-H, 1990.

Plimpton, George, ed. *Poets at Work: The Paris Review Interviews.* London: Penguin, 1989.

_____. *Women Writers at Work: The Paris Review Interviews.* London: Harcourt, 1979.

_____. *Writers at Work.* 3rd ser. New York: Viking, 1967.

_____. *Writers at Work.* 4th ser. New York: Viking, 1976.

Waldrup, Tom, ed. *Writers on Writing.* New York: Random, 1985.

_____, ed. *Writers on Writing.* Vol 2. New York: Random, 1988.

Woolf, Virginia. *Women and Writing.* Ed. Michele Barrett. New York: Harcourt, 1979.

_____. *A Writer's Diary.* Ed. Leonard Woolf. New York: Harcourt, 1954.